British Groun[d]
Aircraft o[f the]
1970s and '80s

CHRIS GOSS

Key
Books

HISTORIC MILITARY AIRCRAFT SERIES, VOLUME 8

Contents page: Built in 1981 as a Sea Harrier FRS.1 but converted to an FA.2 in 1987, Harrier FRS.1 XZ499/255 of 809 Sqn is photographed in November 1982. This aircraft joined 809 Sqn in April 1982 and was one of eight flown to Ascension Island, after which it embarked on the ill-fated SS *Atlantic Conveyor* and then flew to HMS *Hermes* to join 800 Sqn. On 22 May 1982, Lt Martin Hale was flying this aircraft and strafed the Argentinean patrol boat *Rio Iguazu*, forcing it to be beached. On 8 June 1982, Lt Dave Smith shot down an A4B Skyhawk of Grupo 5 over Choiseul Sound killing its pilot, Lt Juan Arrarás. This aircraft joined the Fleet Air Arm Museum in 2002.

Published by Key Books
An imprint of Key Publishing Ltd
PO Box 100
Stamford
Lincs PE19 1XQ

www.keypublishing.com

The right of Chris Goss to be identified as the author of this book has been asserted in accordance with the Copyright, Designs and Patents Act 1988 Sections 77 and 78.

Copyright © Chris Goss, 2021

ISBN 978 1 80282 041 6

Typeset by SJmagic DESIGN SERVICES, India.

Contents

Foreword

It is an honour and a privilege to be invited to write a few words to introduce this excellent pictorial record of two of the most significant offensive aircraft in service with the RAF in the 1970s and '80s. My credentials rest mostly on my 2,000 plus hours and three frontline tours on the Jaguar, but I also have a great respect for the iconic Harrier, not least from my role of running the Air Support Operations Centre (ASOC) in Germany, tasking the Harriers in their war role in the early 1980s.

The Harrier is probably the most publicised and photographed military aircraft of the jet age, using its vertical take-off and landing capability very effectively in both land and maritime domains. Besides this unique capability, it shares many similarities with the Jaguar: both were single seat attack/recce aircraft with advanced Head Up Display/Nav displays, and both carried similar weapons. The Harrier came into service a few years before the Jaguar and was prematurely retired a few years after the Jaguar. Besides the Jaguar's important nuclear strike role, each served with distinction in the recce/attack roles in Germany, and on the flanks of NATO during the Cold War, as part of the first line of defence against any attack by the Soviet Union.

I completed my first flying tour in the mid-1970s as a pilot on the Phantom FGR.2 at RAF Coningsby with 41(F) Sqn in the recce/attack roles, and I volunteered for the Jaguar, as all the UK Phantoms were moving to the air defence role, to be replaced by the Jaguar, which was an exciting new project. The Anglo–French Sepecat Jaguar GR.1 single seat and T.2 trainer had just come into service at RAF Coltishall, with 6 and 54 Sqns in the conventional attack role, with a NATO wartime deployment option to Denmark, and at RAF Brüggen with 14, 17, 20 and 31 Sqns in the nuclear strike/attack roles. These were shortly to be followed by 41(F) Sqn at Coltishall, with a NATO deployment option in Norway, and II (AC) Sqn at RAF Laarbruch, both in the recce/attack roles. The Jaguar was exported to Ecuador, India, Nigeria, and Oman. The French also flew the Jaguar in the attack role, extensively in Chad, but with its more rudimentary avionics, it never reached its full potential compared with the UK variant.

Joining II (AC) Sqn at Laarbruch in March 1977, via the Jaguar's 226 OCU at RAF Lossiemouth, I quickly got used to the novel nav/attack system and settled into the routine of MINEVALs and TACEVALs in high readiness for our Cold War tasks. The Adour Mk 102 engines were always working hard to launch the aircraft in our standard fit of 600kg recce pod on the centreline, fuel tanks inboard, and bombs/dispensers outboard, and the Air Traffic Controller often had to lower the barrier at the far end of the runway to enable the aircraft to launch safely on summer days. During this tour, I became the first Electronic Warfare instructor on the squadron, teaching pilots how to interpret the new Radar Warning Receiver equipment, and I also ran a night, low level trial to prove that we could do recce tasks at low level, using the pod's infrared linescan sensor.

Meanwhile, the Harrier GR.3 was based initially at RAF Wildenrath, and then moved further forward to RAF Gütersloh, with 3 (F) Sqn and IV (AC) Sqn. The forward basing was to provide quick reaction Close Air Support to the British and Belgian Corps, which were holding the line in that area against a possible 3 Shock Army advance across the Inner German Border in that area south of Hannover.

From Laarbruch, in 1979, I was posted on promotion to the British Corps Headquarters to run the ASOC and to task the Harrier in its war role. Using their unique V/STOL capability, the Harriers would be deployed east of Gütersloh into secret field sites, from which they could be on target within minutes in defence of the Army. The UK-based Harriers of 1(F) Sqn, and the OCU based at RAF Wittering, were ready to be deployed anywhere in the world on contingency operations, and found themselves in the South Atlantic, alongside their RN Sea Harrier colleagues for the Falklands War in 1982, where they acquitted themselves extremely well.

I was fortunate to be posted back to Laarbruch that year as a Flight Commander on II (AC) Sqn and had the pleasure, in 1983, of flying out to Goose Bay in Labrador with the whole squadron without air refuelling via Lossiemouth, Iceland and Greenland. Such deployments were made easy by the Jaguar's impressive serviceability, which meant that an aircraft very rarely went unserviceable en route. I returned to Laarbruch again in 1987, as OC of the Sqn, tasked with converting the last Jaguar Sqn in Germany to the Tornado recce variant, handing over the squadron in December 1988. The Berlin Wall came down in 1989, and the Peace Dividend saw a reduction in investment in our armed forces, despite the fact that the world was far from stable. There is no doubt in my mind that the deterrent effect of NATO's combat forces in Germany played a major part in convincing the Soviet Union that its posture was unsustainable. The professionalism of the Jaguar and Harrier forces was evident from the excellent scores they consistently earned on TACEVAL, but this was at a cost. The Jaguar and Harrier forces each regularly lost aircraft and pilots, flying to the limits in achieving and maintaining these high standards in aircraft which were a joy to fly, but were in serious need of modernisation. I considered myself fortunate to hand back the same number of pilots and aircraft that I was given when I took command of II (AC) Sqn. I am often asked which of the 110 or so aircraft types I have flown is my favourite. My immediate answer is always the Jaguar. It was like putting on a glove and was naturally at home at very low level, which was the domain we had to exploit in the 1970s and '80s. I am not alone – you will never meet an unhappy Jaguar pilot, despite all the jokes about power and bowls of milk!

I hope you enjoy this pictorial record of the Harrier and Jaguar over this period, which celebrates the achievements of two superb aircraft much loved by pilots and groundcrew alike.

Air Marshal Philip Sturley CB MBE BSc FRAeS

Introduction

This book is the third in a series devoted to British combat aircraft of the 1970s and 1980s, two decades that were destined to be the last 20 years of the Cold War. This book, like the others before it, is a tribute to the late David Howley, who passed away in 2015. David's dedication to recording aircraft throughout his RAF career resulted in an extensive collection of slides and photographs of aircraft, predominantly British, all of which he generously passed to me.

The first book in the series covered British fighters, namely the Lightning and Phantom, and the second the pure bombers, namely the Buccaneer and Vulcan. This book covers the ground attack/ tactical reconnaissance aircraft, focusing on the Jaguar and Harrier. The Jaguar was a hard-working aircraft, which, should the need arise, would be in the forefront of countering any Soviet advances, normally at low level. As a result, a number were lost in training accidents. During my research into the Jaguar photographs, the name of one of the pilots who lost his life in one such accident came up; this pilot was on my Officer Training Course, which graduated in March 1980, and was also at 4 Flying Training School at Linton-on-Ouse at the same time as me.

As this book concerns the '70s and '80s, only the earlier Marks of Harrier are covered, namely the GR.1 and GR.3 and the fighter/reconnaissance and strike Sea Harrier. I have fond memories of this type, as I held on IV (AC) Sqn at RAF Gütersloh as its intelligence officer in the summer of 1980 between flying training courses. As a reminder of those times, writing this book has brought back both good and sad memories. Hopefully, for the reader, this book will only bring back happy memories of two well-loved aircraft.

I would like to thank Air Marshal Phil Sturley, former Commanding Officer of II (AC) Sqn, for agreeing to write the foreword, Andy Thomas for his advice and Bernd Rauchbach for checking the captions for me. I would also like to thank the late Richard Leask Ward, another great aviation photographer and record keeper, some of whose photographs are believed to have ended up in this collection. Finally, this book is especially dedicated to the late David Howley, without whose generosity I would not have had access to so many photographs of Jaguars and Harriers.

Chris Goss
Marlow 2021

Chapter 1

Jaguar

Jaguar S.06 first flew on 12 October 1969, and in 1972, was at the Aeroplane and Armament Experimental Establishment (A&AEE) Boscombe Down. On 11 August 1972, a ruptured fuel line caused an engine fire on start up and the aircraft was severely damaged. It was then used for ground instructional duties at RAF Lossiemouth and at Warton, and the nose eventually ended up with 1343 (East Grinstead) Sqn Air Training Corps. It is now in the Boscombe Down Aviation Collection.

Photographed in May 1974, this very clean Jaguar GR.1 was flying from RAF Lossiemouth with 226 Operational Conversion Unit (OCU). Other photographs show the serial as possibly being XX763 (but this aircraft did not first fly until 1975) or XX783.

A Jaguar T.2 on static display. Apart from starting with XX, the full serial cannot be discerned.

With the rear canopy open for comfort, an unidentified Jaguar T.2 taxies out. In the background, a Britannia is being loaded with freight.

Jaguar XZ106 started life in 1976 with II (AC) Sqn RAF Laarbruch as a GR.1A. In 1990, it took part in Operation *Granby*, flying 35 missions before returning to be upgraded to a GR.3A, after which it flew with 41 (F) Sqn at RAF Coltishall. It took part in Operation *Deliberate Force* over Bosnia in 1994, but was retired in May 2005, after which it was put up for disposal. It was obtained by the RAF Manston History Museum in 2008, where it still resides today.

Jaguar GR.1 XX122 of 54 (F) Sqn first flew in 1974. On 2 April 1982, this aircraft was No 3 of a three-aircraft formation tasked with carrying out weapons training on the Holbeach Range, Norfolk. The weather was hazy, and it is believed that the pilot, on exchange from the Royal Norwegian Air Force, became disorientated and was killed when the aircraft crashed into The Wash, near Hunstanton.

Photographed at RAF Gütersloh in July 1975 is Jaguar GR.1 XX756 of 14 Sqn, then based at RAF Brüggen. It first flew in March 1975 and was then taken on charge by the RAF in April 1975. During its service career, it also flew with 6, 20, 41 (F) and 54 (F) Sqns. It then became a ground instructional airframe and was recorded as being with the Defence College of Aeronautical Engineering (DCAE), which existed in 2004–09, but is now known as the Defence School of Aeronautical Engineering (DSAE) at RAF Cosford, and was last recorded there in October 2019.

Although just outside the date range of this book, this is a Jaguar GR.3 of the Strike Attack Operational Evaluation Unit. It is photographed in June 2004 alongside a Harrier GR.7 of the same unit at RAF Waddington. It carries a dummy AIM 9L air-to-air missile over wing and, outside the fuel tank, an AN/ALQ 101 Electronic Countermeasures pod. Three years after this photograph was taken, the Jaguar was taken out of service; the date was initially expected to be October 2007, but it was then brought forward to April 2007.

Jaguar GR.1 XX741 of 54 (F) Sqn is seen at RAF Lossiemouth in 1977. This aircraft joined 226 OCU in November 1974, serving then with 54 (F) and 6 Sqns, and ending its operational career with 16 (R) Sqn in January 1994, by which time it had been modified to a GR.1A standard. It was then bought by Everett Aero at Sproughton in Suffolk, but, in October 2009, it was obtained by the Bentwaters Cold War Museum in Suffolk. Over the next ten years, volunteers succeeded in restoring it, eventually enabling it to move under its own power in August 2019. Then, in March 2020, XX741 achieved full power and reheat, and carried out two fast runs on the Bentwaters runway before deploying its brake parachute.

Seen at RAF Abingdon in September 1983 is Jaguar GR.1 XX965, coded AM, of 14 Sqn. This aircraft first flew in November 1975 and then joined 14 Sqn at RAF Brüggen. By June 1990, it had been converted to a GR.1A and was with 226 OCU, later 16 (R) Sqn, at RAF Lossiemouth. It would then become a ground instructional airframe at RAF Cranwell and later the DSAE at RAF Cosford, where it still exists in 2021.

Photographed at RAF Mildenhall in May 1989 is Jaguar GR.1A XZ104/EE of 6 Sqn. First flown in February 1976 as a GR.1, it joined II (AC) Sqn at RAF Laarbruch the following month. When the squadron began converting to the Tornado, it was converted to a GR.1A and joined 6 Sqn the month this photograph was taken. By 1997, it was flying with 41 (F) Sqn and would be converted to GR.3A standard before being grounded in July 2005. After this, it went to RAF St Athan for spares recovery and then to DCAE RAF Cosford to be a ground instructional aircraft; it still exists at the DSAE in 2021.

Jaguar GR.1 XX728/EH of 6 Sqn is photographed at RAF Mildenhall in May 1985. Just over five months later, on 7 October 1985, this aircraft was leading a three-aircraft, low-level formation and, during the turn, No 2 aircraft, XX731, collided with XX728. Both aircraft crashed at Hartside Pass, four miles west-southwest of Alston, Cumbria. The pilot of XX731 managed to eject, but the pilot of XX728, who was a contemporary of the author, as mentioned, was sadly killed.

Seen at RAF Fairford in July 1991 is Jaguar GR.1A XZ356/EP of 41 (F) Sqn, camouflaged and equipped for Operation *Granby*, which was involved in the liberation of Kuwait. Note the 33 mission symbols and Mary Rose nose art. It first flew in June 1976 and flew with 17, 20 and 54 (F) Sqns. It was retired from 41 (F) Sqn in February 2006, by which time it had been converted to a GR.3A and is now in private hands in Powys, Wales. This aircraft has been immortalised by Corgi Models, but it is in the markings of 6 Sqn, used during Operation *Granby*.

Jaguar GR.1 XZ363/A of 41 (F) Sqn is seen at RAF Brize Norton in June 1984. On 24 July 2001, this aircraft, still with 41 (F) Sqn, but, by then, converted to a GR.3A standard, flew into high ground near Eagle, Alaska, during Exercise *Cope Thunder*; sadly, the pilot did not survive.

Jaguar GR.1 XX752/GF of 54 (F) Sqn is seen at RAF Mildenhall in June 1984, clearly showing the Sqn badge – yellow and blue chequerboard, and the pilot's name in an unusual script. Later converted to a GR.3A, it still exists at DSAE RAF Cosford.

Jaguar XX765 first flew in June 1975 as a GR.1, after which it flew with 14 (F) and 17 Sqns at RAF Brüggen, before going to 226 OCU at the end of the year. In June 1976, it went into storage. However, two years later, it was flown to British Aerospace in Warton, Lancashire, where it would be modified. This aircraft, which had mechanical rods to move its control surfaces, was modified to be one that was electrically signalled digital fly-by-wire, so as to prove the concept for future aircraft. This photograph was taken at Farnborough in September 1984, by which time much of the testing had been completed. The 'ACT' seen is the abbreviation for Active Control Technology. Two months later, XX765 was put into storage. However, it has been preserved in these colours and can today be seen in the RAF Museum at Cosford.

Pictured is a close-up of the nose of Jaguar XX765 at Farnborough in September 1984, showing the badge of those organisations and companies involved in ACT trials.

Jaguar T.2 XX139/C of 226 OCU is seen at RAF Mildenhall in May 1982. It went to 16 (R) Sqn and was converted to a T.4 standard; today, it is believed to be in storage in Suffolk.

Seen at RAF Finningley in July 1977 is Jaguar GR.1 XX738, in the markings of 6 Sqn. It had first flown almost three years before this, but, in 1979, returned to British Aerospace and was loaned to the Indian Air Force as part of the deal to sell Jaguars to them. It returned to the RAF in 1984, then flying with 54 (F) Sqn and again with 6 Sqn, having been converted to a GR.3A standard. Its final flight was on 18 May 2007 to RAF Cosford, where it was initially used for live aircraft marshal training before becoming a static instructional airframe. It still exists at the DSAE today.

Jaguar GR.1 XZ358/L of 41 (F) Sqn is seen at RAF Brize Norton in June 1982. During Operation *Granby*, this aircraft acquired the name *Diplomatic Service*. Ending its operational career with 41 (F) Sqn, it first went to RAF Cranwell for ground instructional purposes, then to DSAE where, coloured all black, it was used for ground aircraft marshal training. It is still at the DSAE.

Jaguar GR.1 XZ400/GP of 54 (F) Sqn is seen here at RAF Alconbury in August 1982. It first flew in February 1978, before being delivered to the RAF in June 1979. Upgraded to a GR.3A standard and last flown by 41 (F) Sqn, it was obtained by Everett Aero but is now in private hands in Selby, South Yorkshire.

Jaguar XW566 is seen at Farnborough in September 1982. The two-seat trainer was first flown in August 1971 as prototype B.08, the last prototype Jaguar built. For the next 11 years, it was used for development work before moving to the Royal Aircraft Establishment (RAE) at Farnborough, where it was painted in this scheme and continued to fly until 1985, after which it was used for ground trials work. In 2004, it was obtained by the Farnborough Air Sciences Trust, where it can still be found today.

Jaguar GR.1A XZ357/K of 41 (F) Sqn is seen at RAF Abingdon in September 1982. It is now part of the Piet Smits Collection at Baarlo, Holland, and is painted all grey and still in 41 (F) Sqn colours. By the time it was disposed of, it had been upgraded to a GR.3A standard.

Jaguar T.2 XX915 of the Empire Test Pilot's School is seen at RAF Greenham Common in July 1983. On 17 January 1984, Sqn Ldr Tim Allen suffered an engine fire when fuel from failed No 1 engine leaked into No 2 engine and ignited. The pilot ejected successfully, and the aircraft crashed on farmland less than a mile from the Chemical Defence Research Establishment at Porton Down, Wiltshire.

A very clean Jaguar GR.1 XX719/GD of 54 (F) Sqn is seen at RAF Brize Norton in June 1983.

This picture shows a close-up of the 54 (F) Sqn badge on Jaguar GR.1 XX737 at RAF Finningley, in July 1977. In 2005, the aircraft, by this time a GR.3A, suffered a bird strike. Following this, it was bought by Honeywell Aerospace in Phoenix, Arizona.

A Jaguar GR.1 XZ362 in II (AC) Sqn markings is photographed in March 1981. On 24 July 1996, by this time upgraded to a GR.1A and flying with 54 (F) Sqn, this aircraft was taking part in Exercise *Cope Thunder* out of Eielson Air Force Base (AFB) in Alaska. The leader of an eight-aircraft formation that was taking part in air combat with F-16s, the aircraft struck treetops on a wooded ridge 20 miles from Eielson. The aircraft lost its drop tanks, as well as a number of sections forward of the intakes, while the engines ingested large amounts of debris. Still under control, but with one engine failing and the inability to relight it and with other warning captions illuminating, the pilot ejected successfully and without injury.

A fully laden Jaguar GR.1 shows its ability to operate away from established bases. The unit markings and aircraft serial are not clearly visible.

This picture shows a close-up of the tail of Jaguar GR.1 XZ114/B of 41 (F) Sqn at RAF St Athan, in September 1981. This aircraft first flew in April 1976 and joined 41 (F) Sqn the following month. Upgraded to a GR.3A standard, it spent most of its time with 41 (F) Sqn but finished its operational career with 6 Sqn, retiring in April 2006 and being stored at RAF Shawbury. The following year, it moved to DCAE and remains with the DSAE today, still in 6 Sqn markings.

A formation take-off of Jaguar GR.1s of 226 OCU from RAF Lossiemouth.

Jaguar T.2 XX837/Z of 226 OCU is seen on final approach to RAF Lossiemouth. First flown in March 1975, it joined 226 OCU in May 1975, and the aircraft remained with the OCU until being grounded and used for ground instructional duties in 1988. It went initially to 1 School of Technical Training (SoTT) at RAF Halton, and then to 2 SoTT at RAF Cosford, before going to RAF Cranwell and then back to RAF Cosford, where it now resides within the DSAE.

Above: A flypast by Jaguar T.2 XX839/Y of 226 OCU. This aircraft was delivered in May 1975 and is known to have flown with 54 (F) Sqn. In October 1995, the aircraft was the subject of a parliamentary question when, during routine major servicing, small stress corrosion cracks were discovered in the fuselage. It was scrapped in May 2002.

Below: Seen here is Jaguar GR.1 XX762/28 of 226 OCU at RAF Lossiemouth. On 23 November 1979, this aircraft, still with 226 OCU, was acting as a chase aircraft and encountered bad weather. During the pull up, the pilot apparently ejected, possibly believing he was about to hit a hill. The aircraft crashed on the summit of Beinn a' Chleibh, Dalmally, Scotland. The pilot sadly died before he could be rescued.

Two Jaguar GR.1s of 226 OCU at RAF Biggin Hill in May 1980. The nearest aircraft, XX766/14, was taken on strength in July 1975. It later flew with 54 (F) and 6 Sqns before returning to 16 (R) Sqn in July 2003. Three years later, the aircraft went to the DCAE, by which stage it had been brought up to a GR.3A standard.

Jaguar GR.1 XX113/09 of 226 OCU is seen at RAF Waddington in June 1980. On 17 July 1981, during a post-maintenance test flight from RAF Abingdon, this aircraft rolled uncontrollably to the left and the pilot ejected, with the Jaguar crashing southeast of Malvern. The cause for the roll was found to be a loose article jamming the port spoiler Powered Flying Control Unit.

Jaguar GR.1 XX730/EC of 6 Sqn is pictured at RAF Mildenhall in May 1982. First flown in 1974, the aircraft became a ground instructional airframe at RAF Cosford, but it is now at Muzeum Lotnictwa Polskiego at Krakow, Poland.

Jaguar GR.1s XX763/24 and XX113/09 of 226 OCU. Both are getting airborne from RAF Wyton in June 1980.

Jaguar GR.1 XX753/05 of 226 OCU is seen at Royal Navy Air Station (RNAS) Yeovilton in August 1980. Built five years previously, it was retired in 1990 and went into storage at RAF Shawbury. It was later reduced to a nose section, which was used as an RAF recruiting aid. In 2010, the nose was obtained by the Newark Air Museum, where it can be seen today in the markings of 16 (R) Sqn.

Jaguar GR.1 XX740 of 6 Sqn is pictured at RAF Lyneham. This aircraft went to the Royal Air Force of Oman and was last recorded in storage at Thumrait in 2007.

The badge seen on Jaguar GR.1 XX768/14 of 226 OCU, pictured at RAF Coningsby in July 1979, is of the OCU's second squadron. On 29 September 1982, this aircraft, then flying with 17 Sqn, suffered the fatigue failure of a low-pressure compressor that ruptured fuel lines, which then led to an engine fire as the aircraft was on approach to RAF Brüggen. Wg Cdr Malcolm Lovett, OC Operations Wing at RAF Brüggen, ejected successfully and the aircraft crashed at Heinsberg-Randerath.

Left: Seen getting airborne from RAF Lossiemouth is Jaguar GR.1 XX748/20 of 226 OCU. This aircraft first flew in December 1974 and joined 226 OCU in February 1975. It then flew with 54 (F) Sqn and took part in Operation *Granby* in 1991, by which time it had been upgraded to a GR.3A. It then flew with 54 (F) Sqn and finally with 6 Sqn, before being retired in May 2007. It has been a ground instructional airframe at RAF Cosford since then.

Below: Jaguar GR.1 XX758/18 of 226 OCU is seen at RAF Lossiemouth. On 18 November 1978, this aircraft flew into a hillside in a snowstorm 14 miles northwest of Dingwall, Ross and Cromarty; sadly, the pilot did not survive.

Jaguar GR.1 XX755/08 of 226 OCU is seen overhead at RAF Lossiemouth. On 10 December 1979, this aircraft collided with Jaguar GR.1 XX749, also of 226 OCU, during a four-aircraft formation training flight and both aircraft crashed at Lumsden, Aberdeenshire. Both pilots managed to eject, but the pilot of XX749, sadly, did not survive.

Right: Jaguar GR.1 XX114/02 of 226 OCU. On 19 September 1983, this aircraft, flown by Fg Off Iain McLean, was on final approach to RAF Lossiemouth when the pilot noticed a flock of birds, forcing him to overshoot – only to fly into another flock of birds! With both engines losing power, the pilot was forced to eject safely at 100ft.

Below: A pair of Jaguar GR.1s of 226 OCU are seen overhead at RAF Lossiemouth.

Jaguar GR.1 XX108 was the first production GR.1 and first flew in October 1972, after which it became a trials aircraft and demonstrator. This photograph was taken at Farnborough in September 1978, but, the following year, it suffered a nose wheel collapse at the Paris Air Show. Repaired, it was upgraded to a GR.1B standard in 1976 and was retired in 2002, after which it was acquired by the Imperial War Museum and can be seen on display at Duxford in Cambridgeshire.

Also at Farnborough in September 1978 was Jaguar XX766/14 of 226 OCU, seen here as a static display. It is now at DSAE, having been brought up to a GR.3A standard.

Seen landing at RAF St Athan in September 1978 is Jaguar GR.1 XX750/22 of 226 OCU. On 7 February 1984, then flying with 14 Sqn, this aircraft was taking part in the *Red Flag* exercises. Having been picked up by ground radar, the pilot apparently lost control and took evasive action; the aircraft crashed on the ranges 90 miles northwest of Nellis AFB in Nevada. The pilot did not survive.

Jaguar GR.1 XZ395 of 54 (F) Sqn is seen at RAF Greenham Common in June 1979. On 22 August 1984, flying the aircraft with 54 (F) Sqn, pilot Sqn Ldr John Froud was forced to eject 20 miles east-northeast of Cromer following loss of control because of excessive rudder movement. The reason for this movement was not established.

Jaguar GR.1 XX742 of 6 Sqn is pictured at RAF Luqa, Malta, in July 1978. On 19 April 1983, this aircraft, still with 6 Sqn, was taking part in Air Combat Training over the North Sea when the pilot, Fg Off Joseph Jackson, was unable to recover from a roll to starboard, possibly caused by the disconnection of the roll control system. The pilot ejected successfully, and the aircraft crashed into the sea 40 miles off Bacton, Norfolk.

On static display at RAF Binbrook in August 1978 is Jaguar GR.1 XX747/17 of 226 OCU. Delivered to the RAF in December 1974, it became another instructional airframe at the end of its flying life. It is known to have been at RAF Cranwell and Cranfield before being sold to Jet Art Aviation in March 2019, where it is again on sale.

Jaguar GR.1 XX110 of 6 Sqn was delivered to 226 OCU in April 1976, after which it flew with 6 Sqn. This photograph was taken at RAF Wyton in June 1980. Retired five years later, it went into storage at RAF Shawbury, before moving to RAF Cosford in 1989 to be used for ground training. It is now on display at RAF Cosford as a Gate Guardian, albeit nowhere near the main gate.

Jaguar XZ117/E of 41 (F) Sqn at RAF Lyneham in 1977. It joined this squadron in May 1975 and later flew with 54 (F) and 6 Sqns. In 2004, it was the 16 (R) Sqn display aircraft, but the following year it went back to 54 (F) Sqn and, finally, 6 Sqn. Having been converted to a GR.3A standard, it was flown to RAF Cosford in 2007 and is still a ground instructional aircraft at the DSAE in 2021.

Unfortunately, the serial of this 20 Sqn Jaguar GR.1 cannot be seen. It is photographed at RAF Wildenrath in June 1978, during the 2 Allied Tactical Air Force Tactical Weapons Meet 1978.

Jaguar GR.1s XX738 and XX742 of 6 Sqn, seen here about to get airborne from RAF Luqa in July 1978.

A picture of the tail of Jaguar GR.1 XZ359/M of 41 (F) Sqn, taken at RAF Finningley in July 1977. On 13 April 1989, this aircraft, then a GR.1A and still with 41 (F) Sqn, flew into 500ft high, fog shrouded cliffs above Lumsdaine Beach, northwest of St Abbs Head, Berwickshire, while descending to low level through cloud; sadly, the pilot did not survive.

Jaguar GR.1 XZ389/CN of 20 Sqn is seen alongside Vulcan B.2A XH559 of 35 Sqn at RAF Finningley in July 1977. While the Vulcan was scrapped just under five years later, the Jaguar is still in existence at the DSAE.

Alongside the other side of Vulcan XH559 is Jaguar GR.1 XZ387/DN of 31 Sqn. On 12 September 1990, this aircraft, by then a GR.1A and flown by 54 (F) Sqn, flew into the sea in the Solway Firth five miles off Southerness Point, Dumfries and Galloway. It was one of four aircraft preparing for deployment on Operation *Granby*. The pilot did not survive.

A close-up of the intake flash on Jaguar GR.1 XZ388/BK of 17 Sqn at RAF Finningley in July 1977. This aircraft was lost while flying with 14 Sqn on 1 April 1985. During let down to the Munsterlager Range in Germany, the pilot became distracted in the cockpit and when he looked out, the aircraft was in a banked turn close to the ground and when it was clear that, despite full power, the aircraft would hit the ground, the pilot ejected.

The intake flash seen on Jaguar GR.1 XZ387/DN of 31 Sqn at RAF Finningley in July 1977.

The intake flash seen on Jaguar GR.1 XZ374/CA of 20 Sqn at RAF Conningsby in June 1977. First flown in December 1976, it would appear that much of its time was spent with 20 Sqn as, in June 1984, the squadron began converting to the Tornado. This aircraft is then reported as being with 14 Sqn in 1985, after which it went into storage at RAF Shawbury. In 1989, it moved to RAF Cosford, where it is still today, in 14 Sqn markings.

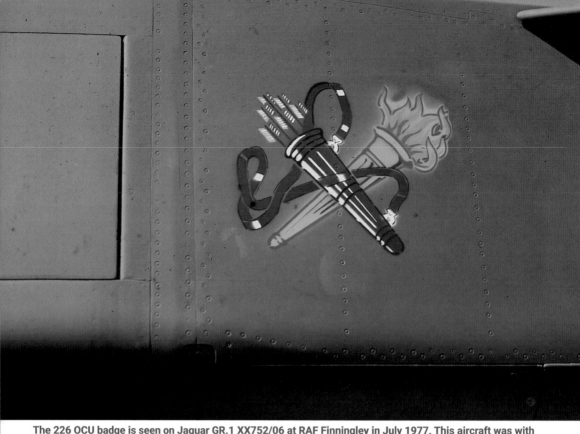

The 226 OCU badge is seen on Jaguar GR.1 XX752/06 at RAF Finningley in July 1977. This aircraft was with 54 (F) Sqn in 1984 and later converted to a GR.3A. It still exists as a ground instructional aircraft at DSAE.

The intake flash on a Jaguar GR.1 of 14 Sqn at RAF Abingdon in June 1977. The serial of this aircraft was not recorded.

The intake flash on Jaguar GR.1 XZ391/11 of II (AC) Sqn, seen at RAF Finningley in July 1977. Joining the RAF in July 1977, it also flew with 31 and 54 (F) Sqns and was converted to a GR.3A. It went into storage at RAF Shawbury in April 2006, but in the following years joined the DCAE (now DSAE) where it is still today, in 6 Sqn markings.

A clearer view of Jaguar GR.1 XZ391/11, showing the precise location of the intake flash.

A Jaguar GR.1 is pictured carrying out a flyby while retracting its undercarriage. Note the first letters of the serial are XX, and the Jaguar flash on the tail.

Here, a Jaguar GR.1 of 226 OCU is displaying at RAF Greenham Common in August 1976, this time with undercarriage down.

Jaguar GR.1A XZ104/M of 41 Sqn at RAF Fairford in July 1989. This aircraft joined II (AC) Sqn in March 1976 as a GR.1, then converted to a GR.1A and flew with 6 Sqn. In 1997, it was with 41 (F) Sqn and was converted to a GR.3A standard. Grounded in 2005, it arrived at RAF Cosford in October 1985 and is still there in 2021.

Delivered to the RAF in December 1974, Jaguar T.2A XX830 is seen here in the distinctive markings of the Empire Test Pilot's School. This aircraft also flew with 226 OCU with the tail letter R. Its nose section is now on display at the City of Norwich Aviation Museum.

Seen at RAF Wyton in August 1986 is Jaguar T.2A XX146/GS of 54 (F) Sqn. Built in 1974, it was later converted to a T.4 and obtained by the Bradwell Bay Military and Science Museum near Southminster in Essex. This museum is now closed but, as of June 2021, XX146 is still believed to be at this former wartime airfield.

Jaguar GR.1A XX119/01 of 226 OCU at RAF St Mawgan in August 1986. It was delivered to the OCU in December 1973, and by 1981 was with 54 (F) Sqn. Two years later, it was with the A&AEE for trials work, coming back to 226 OCU in May 1986, and then 16 (R) Sqn. Converted to a GR.3 standard in 1998, it then went back to Boscombe Down before going to 54 (F) Sqn. Subsequently converted to a GR.3A, it remained with 54 (F) Sqn, before finally finishing with 6 Sqn. It would be given a leopard-style paint scheme and would be the last Jaguar to retire in July 2007, when it was flown to RAF Cosford, where it still remains today.

Jaguar GR.1A XZ355/J of 41 (F) Sqn seen at RAF Abingdon in September 1987. First flown as a GR.1 in 1976, it was upgraded to a GR.3A standard and was later bought by a private collector in Greece. The badge on the tank would indicate it has been 'zapped' by the RF-4E Phantom-equipped Aufklärungsgeschwader 51 Immelmann, which was based at Bremgarten.

Jaguar GR.1A XX955/GK of 54 (F) Sqn is photographed at RAF St Mawgan in May 1989. Delivered to the RAF in October 1976, in May 1988 it went into storage at RAF Shawbury. It was then purchased by Everett Aero, who then sold the aircraft to Flugausstellung Peter Junior in Hermeskeil, Germany, where apparently it is still on display in 2021.

Seen at Ramstein AFB in Germany during Tactical Air Meet 80 is one of the participants – a Jaguar GR.1 of 31 Sqn.

Getting airborne from Farnborough in May 1987 is a Jaguar GR.1, identified as being from II (AC) Sqn by the tail and intake markings.

A four-ship formation from II (AC) Sqn, pictured displaying over Farnborough in May 1987.

Jaguar GR.1A XZ109/29 of II (AC) Sqn at Hurn Airport in May 1986. Taken on strength in April 1976, it would eventually be converted to a GR.3A standard. Grounded in 2006, the following year it went to the DCAE and is still at the DSAE in 2021, albeit in 6 Sqn markings.

Also seen at Hurn in May 1986 was Jaguar GR.1A XX723/07 of 226 OCU. Joining the RAF in April 1974, it was first assigned to the OCU but then went to 54 (F) and 6 Sqns before returning to the OCU, which then became 16 (R) Sqn. It went into storage at RAF Shawbury in 2006 but soon afterwards went to the DCAE.

Jaguar GR.1A XX117/A of 226 OCU was built in 1973, but in 1979 it transferred to the Indian Air Force, returning to the RAF in February 1984. Upgraded to a GR.3A standard, it was retired in 2005 but, like many other Jaguars, still remains today at the DSAE.

Jaguar GR.1 XZ116/D of 41 (F) Sqn at RAF Abingdon in September 1983. On 17 June 1987, this aircraft, by then a GR.1A standard, was one of a pair flying together on a low-level training flight over the Lake District. The two aircraft flew low over Derwent Water from west to east and began a climb to avoid high ground to the east. XZ116, the lead aircraft, was then hit head on by Tornado GR.1 ZA493 of 20 Sqn, which had flown down Thirlmere and was making a climbing turn east over the high ground between Thirlmere and Derwent Water. The Jaguar pilot was probably killed instantly; the aircraft then exploded, the wreckage falling around Castlerigg Fell. The crew of the Tornado ejected and landed safely, with the aircraft crashing next to the main Borrowdale road, heading south out of Keswick.

Being towed into position at RAF Coltishall in September 1980 is Jaguar GR.1 XZ114/B of 41 (F) Sqn. Delivered to the RAF in May 1976, it joined 41 (F) Sqn, with which it remained for much of its career. In 1986, it sported a roughly applied temporary snow camouflage scheme, and in 1991 it was painted desert pink for Operation *Granby*, after which it reverted to a light grey finish. By 2005, it was with 6 Sqn and, after retirement in April 2006, first went to RAF Shawbury but now exists at the DSAE.

Photographed at RAF Marham in April 1983 is Jaguar GR.1 XZ396/EM, which, at this time, was with 6 Sqn. Later upgraded to a GR.1A and then GR.3A, it was retired to RAF St Athan in 2005 for spares recovery and was bought by Everett Aero. In 2014, it went to Pima Air and Space Museum at Davis-Monthan AFB at Tucson, Arizona.

Jaguar GR.1 XZ360/Y of 41 (F) Sqn at RNAS Yeovilton in August 1981. Delivered as a GR.1 in 1976, it was later modified to a GR.3A. After being grounded, it was obtained by Everett Aero and stored at Bentwaters in Suffolk. However, in August 2019, it was moved to Teesside Airport near Darlington to be used for fire training.

Jaguar T.2 XX140/D of 226 OCU is seen at RAF Lossiemouth. After retirement, it was obtained by Everett Aero but is now in private hands near Selby, South Yorkshire.

Another 226 OCU Jaguar T.2 at RAF Lossiemouth was XX141/E. After service with 16 (R) Sqn, it ended up at DSAE, where it still is in 2021.

Believed to have been photographed at RNAS Yeovilton in August 1979 is Jaguar GR.1 XX754/23 of 226 OCU. On 13 November 1990, this aircraft, by then a GR.1A, was detached on Operation *Granby* and, during a formation join-up on a low-level training sortie, flew into a ridge 100 miles south of Bahrain; sadly, the pilot failed to eject.

Jaguar GR.1 XZ386/AJ of 14 Sqn seen at RAF Finningley in July 1977. Almost ten years later, on 23 June 1987, this aircraft, by then a GR.1A with 226 OCU, was acting as an aggressor with two other Jaguars, during which the pilot had to bunt and roll to port to avoid a collision. He then entered the slipstream of one of the other Jaguars and had to take further avoiding action, but control was lost, and the aircraft crashed at Aberedw, three miles southeast of Builth Wells in Powys. Sadly, the pilot lost his life.

Photographed in August 1976, Jaguar GR.1 XZ358 streams its brake parachute. No squadron markings can be seen, but this aircraft ended its career with 41 (F) Sqn and still exists at DSAE.

Looks can be deceptive. Jaguar GR.1A XX732 was lost in an accident on 27 November 1986, when a USAF exchange pilot with 226 OCU crashed into Stock Hill, Eskdalemuir Forest, 11 miles southwest of Hawick in the Borders; the pilot was killed. This photograph taken at RAF Abingdon in June 1977 is of a plastic replica of a GR.1 in 54 (F) Sqn markings, used by the RAF as a static display.

Chapter 2

Harrier

Seen onboard HMS *Ark Royal* in March 1963 is Hawker P.1127 vertical/short take-off and landing (V/STOL) serial XP831, the first prototype. This aircraft, flown by test pilot Bill Bedford, flew its first untethered hovering flight at the airfield at Dunsfold in Surrey on 19 November 1960. This aircraft can be seen today in the Science Museum in London.

Above: Photographed at RAF Upavon in Wiltshire in June 1962, XP831 was coloured pale cream with black intakes. On the nose was written Hawker P1127.

Right: A Hawker Siddeley Aviation Ltd photograph shows the ability of the aircraft to take off and land vertically. The prototype, P.1127, led to the Kestrel FGA.1, essentially an improved P.1127, of which nine were built. The first aircraft flew in March 1964. In 1967, the RAF placed an order for what was designated the Harrier GR.1.

The last of six pre-production Harriers, Harrier GR.1 XV281 first flew on 14 July 1967, after which it was used for test and development work. It then became a ground instructional airframe for British Aerospace at Preston, before being sold. It currently resides at the South Yorkshire Aircraft Museum at Doncaster.

This aircraft is believed to be Harrier GR.1 XV281, however, in this photograph, the aircraft is fitted with a 30mm ADEN cannon pod and Matra rocket pods for the 68mm Société Nouvelle des Etablissements Edgar Brandt rockets, more commonly known as SNEB rockets.

In October 1967, a Harrier GR.1 demonstrated its ability to land on the Marina Militare helicopter carrier *Andrea Doria* at La Spezia. However, an Italian law dating from 1937 prohibited fixed-wing aircraft being operated by their navy; this law was changed in 1989, after which orders were placed.

Photographed at RAF Biggin Hill in September 1971 is Harrier GR.1 XV752. The badge on the nose shows a grasshopper, around which is written 'Harrier OCU'. This aircraft first flew in May 1969, after which it went to the Harrier Conversion Team and then, in December 1969, to 1 (F) Sqn at RAF Wittering. In May 1970, it went to the Conversion Unit that would become 233 OCU. Two years later, it was upgraded to a GR.1A and, two years after that, to a GR.3. After a long and varied career, it would eventually be retired in December 1990, by which time it was with IV (AC) Sqn at RAF Gütersloh. For the next five years, it was a static display and ground instructional aircraft at RAF Cosford, before being loaned to 2366 (Bletchley Park) Sqn Air Training Corps. It is now at the South Yorkshire Aircraft Museum.

Harrier GR.1 XV752 taxies out at RAF Biggin Hill in September 1971, clearly showing the Harrier OCU badge.

Seen here is a Harrier GR.1, believed to be serial XV779 in IV (AC) Sqn markings. Delivered to the RAF in May 1970, it would be converted to a GR.3, but, on 16 December 1974, it apparently suffered a hydraulic systems failure and belly landed at RAF Wildenrath. The aircraft became a Gate Guardian at RAF Wittering and now resides in the Harrier Heritage Centre at RAF Wittering.

No serial number is visible on this Harrier GR.1. However, it has the letter G on the tail, the badge of IV (AC) Sqn on the nose and the name of its pilot, Flt Lt John Thorpe, under the cockpit.

Harrier GR.1 XV745, seen here with the flash on the nose of 233 OCU. From left to right, the badge was coloured red/grey/yellow/black, with a black panther's head in the centre. Converted to a GR.3, this aircraft collided with Harrier GR.3 XV754 on 19 January 1976 and crashed near the Little Man Public House, Wettenhall, Nantwich, Cheshire. Sadly, both pilots did not survive.

The badge of 1 (F) Sqn seen on the nose of Harrier T.4 XW271/17 at RAF Finningley in July 1977. Built as a T.2, this aircraft was delivered to 1 (F) Sqn in July 1971, after which it was converted to a T.2A, and then to a T.4A in December 1973. After serving with 233 OCU and 3 and IV (AC) Sqns, it was retired to Royal Navy Air Station (RNAS) Culdrose and, in 2007, moved to Predannack Airfield, where it resided in the fire training dump. In 2012, XW271 was obtained by Everett Aero in Suffolk and, three years later, was sold to Advanced VTOL Technologies in Melbourne, Australia.

The 3 Sqn badge is on the nose of Harrier GR.3 XV751, also seen at RAF Finningley in July 1977. Delivered to the RAF in June 1969 as a GR.1, it was modified to a GR.1A standard and then in 1973 to a GR.3. It flew with all the Harrier squadrons, as well as the RN at RNAS Lee-on-the-Solent and still survives in 2021 at the Gatwick Aviation Museum.

The IV (AC) Sqn badge on the nose of Harrier GR.3 XW768 at RAF Finningley in July 1977. Built in 1971, it was flown to 1 SoTT at RAF Halton in 1992, but is now a range target at RAF Spadeadam in Cumbria.

Seen in a mock hide at RAF Finningley in July 1977 is Harrier GR.3 XV748 of 1 (F) Sqn. Built as a GR.1 and first flown in 1969, it served with 1 (F) Sqn and 233 OCU and had been converted to a GR.3 by 1974, after which it became a ground instruction aircraft at the RAE at Bedford. It was bought by the Yorkshire Air Museum at Elvington from Cranfield University in 2000, and it is still on display in the markings of 233 OCU in 2021.

The 233 OCU badge can be seen on the nose of a Harrier T.2 in August 1974. It has not been possible to identify the location or aircraft serial number.

Harrier GR.3 XW922/49 of 233 OCU at RAF St Mawgan in July 1975. On 19 November 1985, this aircraft was written off when it rolled over on landing at RAF Wittering. It was then used for ground instruction/crash rescue training at RAF Manston, and its burnt remains are now in private hands near Selby in South Yorkshire.

Another Harrier GR.1 seen at RAF St Mawgan in July 1975 was XV804/45 of 233 OCU. Following an emergency landing at RAF Spitalgate, near Grantham in Lincolnshire, on 25 October 1977, the aircraft was assessed as damaged beyond repair, after which it was used for ground instruction at a number of locations. In 2013, it was sold to Everett Aero, who then sold it to Pima Air and Space Museum in Tucson, Arizona.

Above and right: Harrier GR.3 XW922/49 of 233 OCU was one of the display aircraft in the summer of 1975. In this image, it is displaying at RNAS Yeovilton in August 1975.

With the display over, Harrier GR.3 XW922/49 of 233 OCU taxies back in. This photograph was taken at RNAS Yeovilton in August 1975.

Harrier GR.3 XZ133/32 of 233 OCU at RAF Greenham Common in July 1976. Built as a GR.3, this aircraft was just two months old when this photograph was taken. In 1982, it was with 1 (F) Sqn and was operating off HMS *Hermes* and the forward strip at Port San Carlos, flying at least nine sorties between 2 and 14 June 1982. It then served with 3 and IV (AC) Sqn in Germany and, after retirement, went to the Imperial War Museum in Duxford, where it is still on display today.

Harrier GR.3 XV762/44 of 233 OCU at RAF Greenham Common in July 1976. On 19 November 1983, this aircraft, which was then with 1453 Flt, was on a practice fighter evasion sortie and had been bounced by an RAF Phantom. The aircraft then struck the ground under power in a right-hand turn and exploded on Lafonia, south of Goose Green, East Falkland. The pilot, who was on the author's senior flying course at RAF Linton-on-Ouse, did not survive.

Photographed at Farnborough in 1976 is the Hawker Siddeley Aviation (HSA) Harrier Mk 52 demonstrator G-VTOL, which also had the military serial ZA250 (allowing the aircraft to legally carry munitions). It first flew in September 1971, and its career came to an end on 19 February 1986, having made 1,389 flights and flown for a total of 721 hours and 33 minutes all around the world. It is now on display at the Brooklands Museum in Surrey.

Seen at Farnborough in September 1978, with garishly coloured inert munitions, is Harrier GR.3 XV789/F of IV (AC) Sqn. This aircraft deployed to RAF Ascension Island on 3 May 1982, flown by Wg Cdr Peter Squire, OC 1 (F) Sqn (later to be Chief of the Air Staff), staging through Banjul. Having been delivered in June 1970, it is believed to have been scrapped at RAF Brüggen in 1996.

The refuelling of a Harrier GR.3 of 1 (F) Sqn, photographed between February and March 1985. The serial of the aircraft is unknown.

Left: Photographed between February and March 1985, the 1 (F) Sqn GR.3 is ready to receive fuel.

Below: Ready to refuel one of 1 (F) Sqn's two-seat aircraft, pictured between February and March 1985.

Harrier GR.1 XW769/A of IV (AC) Sqn at Hurn Airport on 31 May 1986. Just under a month later, on 28 June 1986, this aircraft crashed during an air display at Chièvres in Belgium. Sadly, the RAF Germany Harrier Display pilot did not survive the ejection.

Harrier XZ132/04 of 1 (F) Sqn at RAF Brize Norton in June 1986. Delivered to the RAF in 1976, it flew with all RAF Harrier squadrons and both deployed flights. It also deployed to RAF Ascension Island in May 1982, but it was grounded owing to a serious fuel leak that necessitated it being brought back to the UK; it eventually made it onto 1453 Flt at Port Stanley later that year. In 1990, it became a ground instructional aircraft at RAF Cranwell, before being acquired by Jet Art Aviation Ltd in 2014. As of April 2019, it was believed to be in private hands in the Gloucester area.

Harrier T.4A XZ445/Q of 233 OCU at RAF Abingdon in September 1986. Built in 1979, it would transfer to the RN and fly with 899 Sqn as a T.4A(N). On 23 February 1996, this aircraft crashed during a training exercise near Churchstanton in Somerset, 30 minutes after taking off from RNAS Yeovilton. Both the pilot and passenger failed to eject.

Harrier GR.3 XZ133 of 1 (F) Sqn is seen in temporary winter camouflage. This aircraft was with 1 (F) Sqn in 1982 and operated off HMS *Hermes* and the forward strip at Port San Carlos during the Falklands War. It then served with 3 and IV (AC) Sqn in Germany and is now at the Imperial War Museum in Duxford; this photograph was taken in November or December 1988, location unknown.

Taken in November or December 1988, this Harrier T.4 XW934, also of 1 (F) Sqn, is sporting the same temporary winter camouflage. This aircraft first flew in October 1973 and at the end of its service life in 1990, was flown at RAE Farnborough where it was used for electromagnetic compatibility tests. In August 2009, it was donated by QinetiQ to the Farnborough Air Sciences Trust where it still remains today

Harrier GR.3s XV759/H and XV741/I of 233 OCU at Middle Wallop airfield in July 1988. XV759 was built as a GR.1 and first flew in September 1969; it was later converted to a GR.3. It went into storage at RAF St Athan in 1989, but the nose still exists in private hands in Hertfordshire. XV741 first flew in August 1968, and, on 5 May 1969, this aircraft was flown by Sqn Ldr Tom Lecky-Thompson between London and New York to commemorate the 50th anniversary of the first transatlantic crossing. He completed the flight, which started from a coal yard near St Pancras Station and finished on a pier in the Hudson River, in 6 hours 11 minutes and 57 seconds. Converted to a GR.3, the aircraft then went to the RN's School of Flight Deck Operations at RNAS Culdrose, and, in 2008, was recorded as being with the HMS Sultan Defence School of Maritime Engineering. It was later purchased and restored by Jet Art Aviation and is now on display at the Brooklands Museum.

Another Harrier GR.3 that can be seen in a museum in 2021 is XV744/O of 233 OCU, seen here at RAF Mildenhall in May 1988. This aircraft was flown from New York to London in May 1969 by Flt Lt Graham Williams, following Sqn Ldr Tom Lecky-Thompson as he flew from London to New York in XV741. It was purchased by the Tangmere Military Aviation Museum in West Sussex, where it still can be seen today.

Harrier GR.3 XV810 of 233 OCU at RAF Fairford in July 1987. Delivered to the RAF in April 1971, it was withdrawn from service in 1989. Its nose section is now in private hands at Walcott in Lincolnshire.

Harrier GR.3 XZ969 of IV (AC) Sqn at RAF Fairford in July 1987. Assigned to the School of Flight Deck Operations at RNAS Culdrose, it was left to rot away at Predannack airfield and was still recorded as being there in September 2020.

The history of Harrier GR.3 XZ997/E, seen here with 223 OCU at RAF Mildenhall in May 1987, is well known. Delivered to IV (AC) Sqn in February 1982, two months later it was transferred to 1 (F) Sqn and, on 18 May 1982, Sqn Ldr Jerry Pook landed it on HMS *Hermes*, after which it took a very active part in the air war over the Falkland Islands. It returned to RAF Wittering later in the year and then returned to IV (AC) Sqn, before rejoining 1453 Flt in June 1984. Its last flight was 21 August 1990, after which it went to the RAF Museum.

Harrier T.4 XW927/Q was originally built in 1972 as a T.2, but it was then converted to a T.4, and later a T.4A. On 7 February 1992, it was damaged in a heavy landing at RAF Gütersloh; the aircraft was not repaired and became a ground instructional aircraft, before being struck off charge in November 1996. It then went to the Hermeskeil Aviation Museum, but, four years later, the nose section went to Everett Aero and is now believed to be in private hands in Devon.

Harrier T.4A ZB602/Y of 233 OCU, seen here at RAF Fairford in July 1987, had a very interesting fate. Built in 1983, in September 2002 it went to the Indian Navy and was given the serial IN655.

Harrier GR3. XV738 of 1(F) Sqn at RAF Brize Norton in June 1983. This aircraft, built as a GR.1, was the first production Harrier and was first flown by test pilot Duncan Simpson on 7 March 1967. In 1998, it went to the National Aviation and Transportation Museum of Florida (now the National Naval Aviation Museum) and was given the civil registration N4320W. It was then reported at Arlington Municipal Airport and then the Flying Heritage and Combat Armor Museum at Everett, Washington. As of 2021, the museum is closed and XV738 is no longer listed on their website; the civil registration was cancelled in February 2017.

Harrier GR.3 XZ991/AD of 3 Sqn at RNAS Yeovilton in July 1982. This aircraft had only been taken on strength six months previously. It is now at RAF Cosford, where it was last confirmed at the end of 2019.

Photographed at RAF Wittering is this 233 OCU Harrier GR.3, showing off the array of weapons that could be carried. A precise date and an aircraft serial number are not known.

Harrier GR.3 XV753 of 233 OCU, seen here at Middle Wallop in July 1982, was built in 1969 as a GR.1, after which it was known to have flown with 1 (F) and 3 Sqns, as well as 1417 Flt in Belize. Retired, it first went to 1 SoTT and then, in 1994, to the School of Flight Deck Operations at RNAS Culdrose. Surplus to requirements, it was stored at Predannack airfield before going to the Classic Air Force Museum at Newquay Cornwall Airport. However, when this closed in 2016, XV753 moved to the Cornwall Aviation Heritage Centre.

Also at Middle Wallop in July 1982 was Harrier GR.3 XZ998/J of 233 OCU. Delivered to the RAF just two months before this photo was taken, it is known to have served on 1417 Flt in Belize in 1984 (and again in 1989). By 1993, it was in storage at RAF St Athan, before going to the Central Servicing Development Establishment at RAF Swanton Morley. It is now at the Hermeskeil Aviation Museum in Germany, in the markings of IV (AC) Sqn.

Photographed in a hide at RAF Wyton in June 1980 is Harrier GR.3 XZ964/09 of 1 (F) Sqn. It is now on display in the Royal Engineers Museum at Chatham in Kent, in the markings of 1417 Flt.

Displaying at RAF Wyton in June 1980 is Harrier GR.3 XV748/B of 233 OCU. After its flying career was over, it became a ground instruction aircraft at the RAE at Bedford, but was then bought by the Yorkshire Air Museum at Elvington from Cranfield University in 2000 and was still on display in 2021.

Photographed at RNAS Yeovilton on 4 August 1979 is Harrier GR.1 XV757 of 1 (F) Sqn. On 21 September 1979, this aircraft collided with Harrier GR.3 XZ128; both pilots ejected safely. This aircraft crashed on farmland at Belt Drove near Elm, south of Wisbech in Cambridgeshire.

Spotted languishing in a hangar at RNAS Culdrose in January 1979, this is not a Harrier but Kestrel XS695. One of the nine development aircraft, it first flew on 17 February 1965, after which it was part of the Tri-partite Kestrel Evaluation Sqn at RAF West Raynham. It then went to the Ministry of Aviation, RAE Bedford and A&AEE, but on 1 March 1967, an outrigger sheared on landing at Boscombe Down and the aircraft turned over, trapping Flt Lt Derek Parry. It was then sold to the Ministry of Technology and became a ground test aircraft at A&AEE, before ending up on the scrap dump at Boscombe Down in August 1971. In May 1974, it went to the RN Engineering College at Manadon and then, four years later, to RNAS Culdrose, where it was used for aircraft handling and flight deck procedures training. However, its life did not end there; in 1994, it went to the RAF Museum store at RAF Cardington and then to RAF Wyton and finally RAF Cosford in 2009, where after restoration it was unveiled in 2014 as an exhibit at the RAF Museum, Cosford.

Seen at RAF Valley in August 1979 is Harrier GR.3 XV778/16 of 1 (F) Sqn. Delivered to the RAF in April 1970, it was converted to a GR.3 and flew with 1 (F), 3 and IV (AC) Sqns, 233 OCU and 1417 Flt in Belize. Arriving at 1 (F) Sqn in April 1982, it would become a Falklands War veteran, flying at least nine sorties between 2 and 14 June 1982. However, on 28 July 1982, it was damaged in a storm when a temporary hangar collapsed on it. It was airlifted onto HMS *Invincible* and returned to the UK, where it was repaired and reissued to 3 Sqn. It is believed to have been scrapped in 1995.

Seen at RAF Biggin Hill in September 1982 is Harrier GR.1 XV752/52 of the Harrier OCU, clearly showing its white and yellow badge on the nose.

A shot of the rear of Harrier GR.1 XV752 that shows the red '52', outlined in white, on the top of the tail.

The port side of XV752; the Harrier OCU badge can be seen on both sides of the nose.

Close-up of the gun pod on Harrier GR.3 XW922/45 of 233 OCU at RAF St Mawgan in August 1975.

The shape of things to come. This was shot was taken at Farnborough in 1964.

Above, below and overleaf: A series of photographs showing Harrier GR.1 XV752, by this time in 1 (F) Sqn markings, and showing the versatility of the type.

Seen at RAF Mildenhall in May 1989 is Sea Harrier FRS.1 ZD581/718 of 899 Sqn. Ending its days at RNAS Culdrose, having been upgraded to an FA.2, it currently languishes on Predannack airfield.

Sea Harrier FRS.1 XZ455/715 was taken on charge by the RN in 1979, first joining 700A Sqn for its introduction to service in November 1979, although this unit only existed from June 1979 to March 1980. It then joined 899 Sqn and transferred to 801 Sqn in May 1982; this photograph was taken in November 1982, following its return from taking part in the Falkland Islands air campaign, and suggests that 801 Sqn is the squadron shown here. Converted to an FA.2, it then flew with 899 Sqn and then 801 Sqn. On 14 February 1996, its pilot, Lt R E Phlilips, was unable to maintain balanced flight during a night approach to HMS *Illustrious*, following an operational mission over Bosnia. He ejected and the aircraft crashed into the Adriatic 28 miles northeast of Bari. The remains were recovered and are now believed to be in private hands in South Yorkshire.

Sea Harrier FRS.1 ZA175/004 flew in the Falkland Campaign, and on 21 May 1982, while being flown by Lt Cdr Nigel 'Sharkey' Ward, Commanding Officer of 801 Sqn, shot down a Mirage V Dagger of Grupo 6 north of Port Howard, one of three shot down by Ward and his wingman; all three Argentinean pilots ejected successfully. Converted to an FA.2 in 1996, and following its retirement in 2004, it has resided at the Norfolk and Suffolk Aviation Museum at Flixton.

Sea Harrier FRS.1 XZ439/2 of 899 Sqn is photographed in September 1982. This aircraft had an interesting career; first flown in 1979, it was used for trials work, converted to an FA.2 standard and then disposed of to Everett Aero in Suffolk, who then sold the aircraft to Nalls Aviation Inc and shipped it to the US. By November 2006, it was at St Mary's County Airport, Maryland, and was registered as NX94422. It flew again after being reassembled on 10 November 2007. However, the following day it had to carry out an emergency landing at Naval Air Station Patuxent River, during which the nose wheel collapsed, and the starboard outrigger was damaged. Repaired, it was a popular aircraft at air shows, as it was the first and only privately owned and airworthy Harrier. It was reported as being up for sale in 2020.

Seen at RAF Mildenhall in May 1988 is Sea Harrier FRS.1 ZD613/710 of 899 Sqn. First flown in 1985, it was converted to an FA.2 standard in 1993 and, after serving 800, 801 and 899 NAS, was retired in 2004, after which it was bought privately and located in Leeds. In 2021, it was acquired by Jet Art Aero, who are restoring it ready for sale.

Sea Harrier FRS.1 ZA176/716 of 899 Sqn, photographed here at RAF St Mawgan in August 1986, had a very lucky escape on 6 June 1983. Sub Lt Ian Watson was operating from HMS *Illustrious* off the Portuguese coast but, on returning to the carrier, was unable to locate it and running low on fuel and with his radio not working, headed towards a shipping lane. Spotting the container ship *Alraigo*, he managed to land his aircraft on a container. Four days later, the *Alraigo* docked in Tenerife, together with the Sea Harrier. Converted to an FA.2 standard, it was retired in 2003 but can be seen today at the Newark Air Museum in Nottinghamshire.

A Sea Harrier FRS.1 of 899 Sqn makes a low-level pass at RAF Mildenhall in May 1987.

Another Falklands veteran was Sea Harrier FRS.1 XZ459/716 of 899 Sqn, seen here at RAF Abingdon in September 1983. Flying with 800 Sqn, it flew 49 combat air patrols and four bombing sorties. Converted to an FA.2 standard, it retired in 2002, but in 2007 it was bought by Jet Art Aviation who restored the aircraft before selling it privately. In 2020, the Tangmere Military Aviation Museum purchased it.

Sea Harrier FRS.1 XZ460/710 of 899 Sqn, seen here at RAF Biggin Hill in May 1983, flew with 800 Sqn during the Falklands War. On 8 May 1990, the aircraft crashed into the sea off Cabocogiani, Sicily, shortly after taking off from HMS *Invincible*; sadly, the pilot did not survive.

Harrier T.4N ZB605/718 of 899 Sqn is seen at RNAS Yeovilton in September 1984. On 5 December 2002, still with 899 Sqn but by then converted to a T.8, had taken off from RNAS Yeovilton and was headed for RAF Wittering. On overshooting at Wittering, the aircraft suffered an engine fire. The instructor waited for the student to eject, which the student did successfully, but the instructor, sadly, lost his life.

The nose of Sea Harrier FRS.1 XZ492/23 is pictured at Farnborough in September 1982, having recently returned from the South Atlantic. The kill marking is for an A4 Skyhawk, shot down by Lt Cdr Neil Thomas of 800 Sqn, one of two from Grupo 4 shot down on 21 May 1982. Converted to an FA.2, this aircraft is reported to have crashed into the Sicilian Channel, in the Mediterranean, on 10 December 1996.

Sea Harrier FRS.1 XZ439/2 seen here displaying at Farnborough in September 1982.

Joining the RN in 1982, this Sea Harrier FRS.1 XZ497/4 of 899 Sqn is seen displaying at RNAS Yeovilton in July 1982. Later converted to an FA.2, it was last reported as being at Aerospace Logistics Ltd at Charlwood in Surrey.

With the display over, Sea Harrier FRS.1 XZ497/4 of 899 Sqn comes in to land at RNAS Yeovilton in July 1982.

The tail of Sea Harrier FRS.1 ZA194/251 of 809 Sqn at RNAS Yeovilton in July 1982. On 20 October 1983, this aircraft crashed at West Knighton in Dorset after control problems were encountered. The US Marine Corps Exchange Officer ejected safely.

A line-up of Sea Harrier FRS.1s of 899 and 809 Sqns and a Harrier T.4 of 233 OCU at RNAS Yeovilton in July 1982.

Sea Harrier FRS.1 ZA176/250 of 809 Sqn taxies in at RNAS Yeovilton July 1982, while another FRS.1 comes in to land.

Sea Harrier FRS.2 XZ457/104 of 899 Sqn at Farnborough in September 1980. This aircraft first flew in December 1979 and the following month was delivered to 700A Sqn at RNAS Yeovilton. This then became 899 Sqn. This aircraft was active over the Falkland Islands when, on 21 May 1982, Lt Clive Morrell shot down an A-4Q Skyhawk of CANA 3 Esc near Swan Island; Lt Cdr Philippi managed to eject. He then damaged another aircraft, whose pilot, Lt Arca, then ejected on approach to Port Stanley airport. Then, on 24 May 1982, Lt Cdr Andy Auld shot down two Mirage V Daggers of Grupo 6. On 20 October 1995, a compressor blade broke off on take-off from Yeovilton and the engine exploded. Lt Cdr Clive Baylis immediately made a force-landing, and, as the aircraft rolled towards the barrier on fire, successfully ejected, after which the aircraft was declared surplus and ended up at the Boscombe Down Aviation Collection.

The tail of Sea Harrier FRS.1 XZ454/250N of 800 Sqn, seen here at RNAS Yeovilton in September 1980, showing in great detail the 800 Sqn emblem.

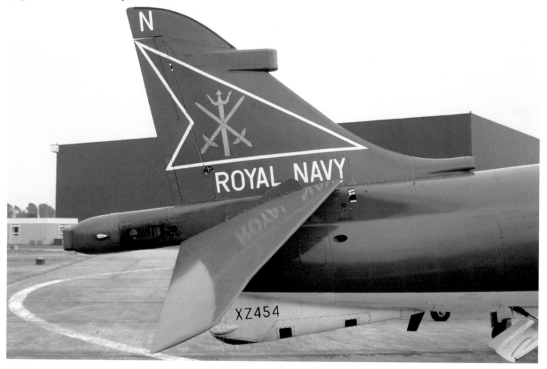

On 1 December 1980, three months after this photograph was taken at RNAS Yeovilton, XZ454 was written off during a flying display over HMS *Invincible*, 25 miles south of Land's End, when it struck the top of the ski ramp while attempting to hover with full fuel. Lt Cdr Mike Blisset ejected and suffered minor injuries. This was the first Sea Harrier to be lost in an accident.

Sea Harrier FRS.1 XZ454/250/N of 800 Sqn seen here displaying at RNAS Yeovilton in September 1980.

Sea Harrier FRS.1 XZ458/251/N of 800 Sqn taxies past at RNAS Yeovilton in September 1980. On 1 December 1984, this aircraft, operating off HMS *Illustrious*, suffered a bird strike northeast of Fort William. The pilot, Lt Collier, ejected successfully and the aircraft crashed at Kilmonivaig Farm, Gairlochy.

Sea Harrier FRS.1 XZ452, in the markings of 899 Sqn, is seen at RNAS Yeovilton in August 1981. On 6 May 1982, this aircraft, then flying with 801 Sqn, was one of a pair of Sea Harriers that took off from HMS *Invincible* on a combat air patrol off the Falkland Islands; neither aircraft returned and both pilots are still missing.

The other Sea Harrier FRS.1 of 801 Sqn, lost on 6 May 1982, was XZ453/105. It is seen here displaying at RAF Greenham Common in June 1981.

Sea Harrier FRS.1 XZ451/100, seen here with 899 Sqn at RAF Greenham Common in June 1981, first flew on 25 May 1979 and was the first Sea Harrier delivered to the RN, joining 700A Sqn in June 1979, after which it went to 899 Sqn and then on to 801 Sqn in April 1982. It was credited with three air combat victories during the Falkland War, plus one damaged. On 1 May 1982, Lt Cdr 'Sharkey' Ward damaged a Beechcraft T-34 C-1 Turbo Mentor of the 4th Naval Attack Sqn, and on the same day, Lt Al Curtis shot down a Canberra B.62 of Grupo 2 north of the Falkland Islands. Then, on 21 May 1982, Lt Cdr Ward shot down a Pucara of Grupo 3 near Darwin and, on 1 June 1982, a C-130 of Transport Grupo 1, 50 miles north of Pebble Island. Serving then with 800 and 801 Sqns, on 1 December 1989, it suffered a control restriction and Lt Mike Auckland successfully ejected off Sardinia.

Sea Harrier FRS.1 XZ494/106 of 899 Sqn is seen at RNAS Yeovilton in August 1981. Delivered in December of the previous year, it would be upgraded to an FA.2; it is owned privately under cover at Castle Farm campsite in Wedmore, Somerset.

The tail of Sea Harrier FRS.1 XZ453/105 of 899 Sqn is seen at RNAS Yeovilton in August 1980. This aircraft was lost with 801 Sqn on 6 May 1982.

In addition to the Rolls Royce badge on the cowling, Sea Harrier FRS.1 XZ453 of 899 Sqn has also acquired the badge of 3 Sqn, one of the RAF's Harrier squadrons.

On static display at RNAS Yeovilton in August 1979 is Sea Harrier FRS.1 XZ451/100/A of 700A Sqn. It went on to have a distinguished war career in the Falkland Islands, before being lost in an accident on 1 December 1989.

Appendix

RAF Jaguar Operational Variants, 1973 to 1990
GR.1
This initial production variant was based on the Jaguar S. It was fitted with Navigation and Weapon Aiming Sub-System (NAVWASS) and Adour Mk 102 engines, which were later replaced by Adour Mk 104s.

GR.1A
This was an upgraded version of the GR.1. It featured NAVWASS II, as well as chaff and flare countermeasures and air-to-air missile capability.

GR.1B
This variant was a GR.1 that had been modified to carry Thermal Imaging Airborne Laser Designator (TIALD) pods.

GR.3
This variant was a GR.1A with upgraded avionics.

GR.3A
This variant provided an avionics upgrade to previous variants.

T.2
A two-seat training version of previous variants.

T.2A
This was a T.2, but with similar upgrades to GR.1A.

T.4
This variant was an avionic upgrade of the T.2A.

Jaguar Operational Squadrons
II (AC) Sqn (Oct 1976–Dec 1988)
6 Sqn (Oct 1974–May 2007)
14 Sqn (Dec 1975–Oct 1985)
16 (R) Sqn (Nov 1991–Mar 2005)
17 Sqn (Feb 1976–Mar 1985)
20 Sqn (Mar 1977–Jun 1984)
31 Sqn (Jun 1976–Nov 1984)
41 (F) Sqn (Apr 1977–Mar 2006)
54 (F) Sqn (Apr 1974–Mar 2005)

226 Operational Conversion Unit (Oct 1974–Nov 1991; it later became 16 (R) Sqn)
Jaguar Conversion Team, RAF Lossiemouth (Mar 1973–Jul 1974)

RN/RAF Harrier Operational Variants, 1967 to 1990
RAF Harrier
GR.1
This was the initial production version and was powered by a Pegasus 6/Mk 101 engine.

GR.1A
This was an upgraded variant of GR.1, with a Pegasus 10/102 engine.

GR.3
This variant was fitted with improved sensors, nose-mounted laser seeker, improved electronic countermeasures and Radar Warning Receiver in the tail. It was powered by Pegasus 11/Mk 103 engines.

T.2
This was a two-seat trainer, fitted with Pegasus Mk 101 engines.

T.2A
This variant was an upgraded T.2, powered by a Pegasus Mk 102 engine.

T.4
This was another two-seat trainer, this time based on the GR.3.

T.4A
This model is the same as a T.4, but it does not have the seeker in the nose.

RN Sea Harrier
FRS.1
The initial production version of this variant was largely based on the GR.3.

FA.2
This was an upgraded FRS.1, modified with Blue Vixen radar and carrying AIM-120 missiles. It was powered by a Pegasus Mk 106 engine. The first aircraft was delivered in 1993.

RAF/RN Harrier Operational Units
RAF
1(F) Sqn (from Jul 1969)
3 Sqn (from Jan 1972)
4 Sqn (from Jun 1970)
20 Sqn (from Dec 1970)
233 Operational Conversion Unit (from Oct 1970)
1417 Flt (Apr 1980–Jul 1993)
1453 Flt (Aug 1983–Jun 1985)
Strike Attack Operational Evaluation Unit (SAOEU)

RN
700A NAS (Jun 1979–Mar 1980)
800 NAS (from Mar 1980)
801 NAS (from Jan 1981)
809 NAS (from Apr 1982)
899 NAS (from Sep 1983)